C000143335

Royal Honiton Lace

Elsie Luxton and Yusai Fukuyama

Royal Honiton Lace

B.T. Batsford Ltd · London

© Elsie Luxton and Yusai Fukuyama
First published in 1988

All rights reserved. No part of this book
may be reproduced, in any form or by any means,
without the permission of the Publisher.

ISBN 0 7134 5764 3

Printed in Great Britain by
Butler and Tanner
Frome, Somerset
for the publisher
B.T. Batsford Ltd
4 Fitzhardinge Street
London W1H 0AH

Contents

Acknowledgements

Our grateful thanks is given to Her Majesty The Queen for her gracious permission to photograph the lace collection at Windsor Castle, and the Royal Christening Robe at Buckingham Palace; Her Majesty Queen Elizabeth the Queen Mother and Sir Alastair Aird, Her Majesty's personal secretary, for permission for Yusai to photograph the Wedding Veil at Clarence House; The Lord Chamberlain, Sir Geoffrey de Bellaigue, and Mrs Harland his private secretary, who have given considerable help and advice; The Lady Roborough, whose help and advice has made this book possible, and Pauline Williams for her help with the typing.

The group and portrait photographs in this book are from the Royal Archives. The detailed lace photographs were taken especially for the book by the Royal photographer, with the exception of the Queen Mother's wedding veil and coronation fan, which were photographed by Yusai Fukuyama. All the photographs now form part of the Royal Archives and are reproduced here by gracious permission of Her Majesty The Queen, with the exception of the following:

Queen Victoria p. 45 (The Press Association)
Jane Bidney p. 88 (Mrs I. Bidney Mansell)
Six Honiton lace handkerchieves p. 89 (Elsie Luxton)
Honiton lace-edged handkerchief p. 93 (Express and Echo Western Times, Exeter)

Preface

Since the interest in lacemaking has grown so much in recent years, Yusai Fukuyama (a friend, past lace student and now my co-author) and I, thought it would be an appropriate time to produce a book showing examples of some of the exquisite Honiton lace belonging to the Royal Family.

Many books have been written describing their other treasures, namely pictures, furniture, jewellery and other works of art, but until now nothing has been written on lace. The Royal Christening Robe is famous worldwide and is indeed a very special item, and it has been a great privilege and pleasure to have been able to view all these lovely pieces of lace. The major items date back to Queen Victoria and her special interest and love of lace.

The photographs are mainly a pictorial record of beautiful lace which will be treasured by future generations, for truly beautiful things do not date but become part of one's heritage. Honiton lace is well known, not only in the United Kingdom, but also throughout the world of fine art and craft. Lacemaking has enjoyed a long and rich tradition in Britain and British lacemaking has developed distinct and individual styles. It has progressed from being concerned solely with technique, to being a creative and expressive art form enjoyed by people of all ages.

We hope this book will be of interest not only to lacemakers and collectors, but also to many other members of the general public. Yusai Fukuyama and I will be donating all royalties from this book to the N.S.P.C.C. (National Society for the Prevention of Cruelty to Children), and Batsford the publishers have also kindly donated £250 to this Charity.

Elsie Luxton
February 1988

A short history of Honiton lace

Honiton lace is generally regarded as the finest, most famous and indeed the most valuable of English laces still being worked today. It was first made in the village of Honiton, Devon in the late sixteenth or early seventeenth century, deriving from a combination of English and European lace techniques. Its specific origins are difficult to ascertain since it is impossible to say when and where lacemaking as we know it actually began, but it is clear that both Flanders and Italy were important areas in the early stages of lacemaking. Venice was undoubtedly one of the larger lacemaking centres at the beginning of the sixteenth century and it was here that many laws were passed to assist lacemakers, whilst large sums of money were granted to teach the craft. Encouragement of this kind was most certainly absent from England during the same period.

Following the flight of the refugees from northern Italy to Flanders in the early sixteenth century, the art gradually spread to many European countries. Lacemaking became particularly popular in Belgium and Holland, whilst in France, lace schools were set up during the reign of Louis XIV and pupils taught by Venetian experts. It was the religious persecution in Flanders and the other Spanish-dominated Low Countries during the second half of the sixteenth century, which forced in excess of 100 000 refugees to flee to England, bringing with them their knowledge and experience of the lace craft. Many of the Flemish people settled in the towns and villages in south and east Devon, where the local communities already were making the English 'bone' lace (so called because fish bones were used instead of bobbins and pins). The Flemish methods of lacemaking were far more advanced and superior to the local techniques, but gradually the two laces combined to give us Honiton lace as we know it today.

Beginning as a rural craft, lacemaking eventually became a cottage industry and grew to become the centre of village life in many communities in the area. The earliest mention of Honiton lace in England is on the tombstone of one James Rodge in St Michael's churchyard, Honiton, 1617; he was a bone lace merchant who bequeathed a large sum of money to the poor of the town. Of the actual lacemakers themselves little record has been kept (how interesting it would be to know the origins of the beautiful collections of lace in our cathedrals and museums). Even some of the workers of the Royal lace shown in this book are not known.

There is no doubt that the height of English lacemaking came in the seventeenth and eighteenth centuries; during the reign of Charles II (1660-85) it is estimated that there were around 25 000 in Devonshire employed as lacemakers. The English were always ready to protect their own trades and crafts, and so various Acts were passed to prohibit the importation of foreign lace in order to encourage the homeworkers. (A copy of the Act of 1697 is shown on p. 10). However, in 1698 it was proposed that the last Act of prohibition be abolished.

Unfortunately a decline in the industry came about at the time of the French Revolution in 1789 when lace was no longer fashionable. Tragically, in 1809 a net-making machine was patented which produced a mesh similar to handmade bobbin net: the number of workers in the Honiton area alone dwindled from several thousand to no more than 300 since the machine lace was quicker and cheaper to produce.

But this was not to last. In the 1830s an order came from Queen Victoria for her wedding dress to be made of Honiton lace. The dress was made in Beer under the supervision of Jane Bidney, but it was with difficulty that she eventually managed to find enough lacemakers to complete the task. The lace on the dress alone cost £1000 – a large sum of money in those days. The result was an exquisitely designed flounce of four yards and a matching veil, one-and-a-half yards square: the workmanship of both was outstanding. It was from this time onwards that lace became fashionable once again and one of the more active persons in the revival was a Mrs Treadwin who, for many years, ran a lace shop in Exeter. She organized her workers, produced better patterns for them and was largely responsible for the excellent design and workmanship of the lace shown by the Devon lacemakers at the Great Exhibition in 1851. Another leading manufacturer of this period was the Tucker family of Branscombe whose workers also produced high-quality lace. It is recorded that around 8000 people were employed in the Honiton lacemaking industry during the mid-nineteenth century but again, towards the end of the century, although the industry was still in existence, demand steadily fell off as machine-made lace took over, and the number of workers dwindled once more.

During the early twentieth century, Devon County Education Authority granted money to help keep the Honiton lace craft alive. Lace classes were held in many Devon schools, but these were discontinued around 1960. However, many adult education classes were beginning to start throughout Devon, and up to the present day, these have been well supported with interest continually growing. Many residential courses have been organized in various parts of the country and abroad since the 1960s, and as England now has a national lace guild with a membership of approximately 9000 people at present, it is evident that the craft is no longer in danger of dying out.

Anno Regni
GULIELMI III.
R·EGIS

Angliæ, Scotiæ, Franciæ & Hiberniæ,

Nono & Decimo.

At the Parliament begun at *Weſtminſter* the Two
and twentieth Day of *November, Anno Dom.* 1695
In the Seventh Year of the Reign of our Sovereign
Lord *WILLIAM* the Third, by the Grace of
God, of *England, Scotland, France* and *Ireland,* King,
Defender of the Faith, *&c.*

And from thence Continued by ſeveral Prorogations and Ad-
journments to the Third Day of *December,* 1697. being
the Third Seſſion of this preſent Parliament.

LONDON,

Printed by *Charles Bill,* and the Executrix of *Tho-
mas Newcomb* deceas'd, Printers to the Kings
moſt Excellent Majeſty. M DC XCVII.

Anno Nono & Decimo

Gulielmi III. Regis.

An Act for rendring the Laws more Effectual for preventing the Importation of Foreign Bone-Lace, Loom-Lace, Needle-work, Point and Cut-work.

Hereas by an Act made in the Thirteenth and Fourteenth Years of the Reign of His late Majesty King Charles the Second, Intituled, An Act Prohibiting the Importation of Foreign Bone-Lace, Cut-work, Imbroidery, Fringe, Band-strings, Buttons and Needle-work, amongst other things, all Foreign Bone-Lace, Cut-Work and Needle-Work are prohibited to be Imported or Sold in the Kingdom of England, or Dominion of Wales, under the Pains, Penalties and Forfeitures

S 2

in the said Act mentioned : And whereas
the Provisions and Penalties in the said
Act have not proved Effectual, but the same
have been Eluded, and great Quantities
of the said Prohibited Goods have been, and
are daily Imported and Sold, to the Im-
poverishment of a great Number of Fami-
lies in England, Whose Livelihood depends
on the making Bone-lace, Needle-work,
Point and Cut-work, and to the great Dis-
couragement of the said Manufactures in
this Kingdom : For Remedy whereof, and
for the more Effectual restraining the Importation and Sale of all Foreign Bone-
lace, Loom-lace, Needle-work, Point and
Cut-work, and for the better Discovery and
Punishment of the same, Be it Enacted by
the Kings most Excellent Majesty, by and
with the Advice and Consent of the Lords
Spiritual and Temporal and Commons in
this present Parliament Assembled, and by
the Authority of the same, That all and
every Person and Persons, who shall from
and after the Five and twentieth Day of
March, One thousand six hundred ninety
eight, Import or cause to be Imported into the Kingdom of England, Dominion or
Wales, or Town of Berwick upon Tweed, or
who shall (from and after the Four and
twentieth Day of December, which shall be
in the Year of our Lord, One thousand six
hundred ninety eight) Sell, Barter, or of-
fer to Sale or Barter, or cause to be Sold
or Bartered, or offered to Sale or Barter, or
who shall knowingly keep in his, her or
their Custody for Sale, or for the Use or

6

Bene=

Benefit of any Importer or Dealer in the said Commodities, any Foreign Bone-lace, Loom-lace, Needle-work, Point or Cut-work, shall forfeit and lose the Sum of Twenty Shillings per Yard for all the said Foreign Bone-lace, Loom-lace, Needle-work, Point and Cut-work so Imported, Sold, Bartered, offered to Sale or Barter, or kept, as aforesaid, together with all the said Goods.

And be it further Enacted by the Authority aforesaid, That the Importation, Selling, Bartering, offering to Sale or Barter, or knowingly keeping for that purpose any Foreign Bone-Lace, Needle-work, Point or Cut-work, shall be, and is hereby Declared to be a Common Nusance, and shall be so Adjudged and Taken to all Intents and Purposes whatsoever; And that the said Prohibited Goods, or any part thereof, shall and may be Seized, and the Offenders Prosecuted by any Person whatsoever; And further, that it shall and may be Lawful, for any Person or Persons, with a Constable or Tythingman, with a Warrant from a Justice of Peace, in the Day time, to enter and go into any House, Shop, Cellar, Warehouse or Room, or other Place Whatsoever, to Search for and Seize any of the Prohibited Goods before mentioned, and in Case of Resistance, to Break open Doors, Chests, Trunks and other Package whatsoever, there to Seize, and from thence to bring any of the Goods Prohibited by this Act; And every Justice of the Peace is hereby Authorized and Impowered to Grant such Warrant to any Credible Per-

C   son

son or Persons, making Oath that he or
they have reason to suspect or believe that
there are some of the said Prohibited Goods
in the Place or Places where he or they in-
tend to Search.

And be it Enacted by the Authority aforesaid, That all Foreign Bone-lace, Loom-
lace, Needle-work, Point and Cut-work,
Seized by virtue of this or any other Act,
shall be carried to the next Custom-house,
and shall not thence be delivered, unless in
order to be Produced at a Tryal, or otherwise Discharged by due Course of Law :
And in case the said Goods so Seized, or a-
ny part thereof, shall be Condemned, then
the same shall be Sold Publickly by Inch
of Candle, whereof Publick Notice in
Writing, by a Paper or Papers Affixed at
the Door of the Custom-house, and other
most publick Place where the said Goods
are Lodged, shall be given at least Ten
Days before the said Sale, and shall not be
delivered to the Buyer or Buyers, until the
said Buyer or Buyers shall have Entred into Bonds, with One or more Sufficient
Surety or Sureties to the Kings Majesty,
His Heirs and Successors, in double the
Value of the said Goods, to Export, or
cause to be Exported, within Six Months
after the Date of the said Obligation, out
of the Kingdom of England, and Dominion
of Wales, all and every part of the said
Foreign Bone-lace, Loom-lace, Needle-
work, Point and Cut-work, so by him,
her or them Bought, as aforesaid, and not
to Import the same, or any part thereof,

7   into

into the **Kingdoms of** England, Scotland **o2 Ireland, o2 into any of His Majesties Domi= nions, in** America, **o2 elsewhere; which said Obligation (upon Certificate of the P2oper Officers of the Customs of the Po2t from whence the said Goods shall be Expo2ted, and also Oath being first made by the said Buyer o2 Buyers, o2 the Person immediate= ly concerned in the Expo2tation thereof, that all and every part of the said Goods were Expo2ted acco2dingly, and not Landed, o2 intended to be Landed again in the King= dom of** England, **o2 Dominion of** Wales, **the Kingdoms of** Scotland **o2** Ireland, **o2 any o= ther part of His Majesties Dominions, in** America, **o2 elsewhere) shall be Uacated and Cancelled, o2 otherwise to be in full Fo2ce and Uirtue; and the said Goods not being so Expo2ted, and the Person o2 Persons, in whose Custody the said Goods are o2 shall be found, shall be again liable to all the Penalties and Fo2feitures in this o2 any other Act mentioned, as if the same had never been Seized.**

P2ovided nevertheless, That if any Bone= lace, Needle=wo2k, Point o2 Cut=wo2k shall be by any Person Seized and Carried to any Custom=house, as Fo2eign, which the said Seizer shall upon further Examination be= lieve to be English, **it shall and may be law= ful fo2 the said Person to take off his Sei= zure, giving Publick Notice in Writing by a Paper o2 Papers affixed at the Doo2 of the Custom=house, and the** Guild-hall, **o2 other most publick place where the said Seizure is made, of the same Seizure, and of the** Quantity

Quantity and Kind of Goods so Seized, to the end that any other Person or Persons may view the said Goods, and Prosecute for the same, if he or they shall think fit; and in Case no Person shall within Ten Days after such Notice, undertake to Prosecute for the same, the same shall be delivered back to the Proprietor thereof, Oath being first made by the said Proprietor or some known Person on his behalf, That the said Goods and every part of them are (to the best of his knowledge and belief) English made, and an Account being also given upon Oath where, and of whom the said Goods were bought, (which said Oath or Oaths any Justice of the Peace for the County, Town or Place where the said Goods so Seized then are, is hereby Impowered and Required to Administer, and to Certifie the same at the next General or Quarter Sessions to be held for such County, Town or Place) and if any Person shall, upon such Oath or Oaths, wilfully forswear him or her self, he or she so Offending, shall be liable to, and suffer all Penalties and Forfeitures Appointed or Inflicted for Perjury by the Common or Statute Laws of this Realm.

And be it further Enacted, That all Officers belonging to the Customs shall be Aiding and Assisting in the effectual Execution of this Act; and that if any such Officer shall willingly or knowingly Connive at the Importation, Delivery or Selling of any Foreign Bone-lace, Loom-lace, Needle-work, Point or Cut-Work, contrary to the true meaning of this Act, the said Officer

shall

shall Forfeit and Lose the Sum of Twenty Pounds, and be for ever uncapable of Serving His Majesty, His Heirs and Successors, in any Office whatsoever.

And be it Enacted by the Authority aforesaid, That if any Question or Doubt shall arise, whether any Bone-lace, Loom-lace, Needle-work, Point or Cut-work, Imported, Found, Seized, Kept, Sold, Bartered, or offered to Sale or Barter, as aforesaid, or any part thereof were Made and Manufactured in Parts beyond the Seas, contrary to this or any other Act, the proof that the said Bone-lace, Loom-lace, Needle-work, Point and Cut-work so Found or Seized, and every part thereof, was Made and Manufactured in the Kingdom of England, Dominion of Wales, or Town of Berwick upon Tweed, shall be only upon the Importer, Keeper, Seller, Retailer, Barterer, him, her or them in Whose Hands or Custody the same shall be found, as aforesaid, and not upon the Informer, Seizer, or Prosecutor, That they were Manufactured beyond the Seas.

And be it further Enacted by the Authority aforesaid, That all and every the Penalties and Forfeitures imposed and incurred by this Act, shall and may be sued for and recovered over and above any Penalties in any former Act in any of His Majesties Courts of Record at Westminster, by Action of Debt, Bill, Plaint or Information, Wherein no Essoign, Priviledge, Protection or Wager of Law shall be Allowed, nor any more than one Imparlance, and the said Penalties and Forfeitures (the reasonable

U

sonable Costs and Charges of such Prose=
cution at Law being first Deducted and
Allowed out of the same to the Pro=
secutor) shall be one Moiety to His Ma=
jesty, His Heirs and Successors, and the
other Moiety to him, her or them that will
Sue for the same.

And it is hereby further Enacted by the
Authority aforesaid, That if any Person or
Persons shall be Sued, Molested or Pro=
secuted for any thing done by Virtue and
in Pursuance of this Act, such Person and
Persons shall and may Plead the General
Issue, and give this Act, and the Spe=
cial Matter in Evidence ; And if after=
wards a Virdict shall pass for the Defen=
fendant or Defendants, or the Plaintiff
shall Discontinue his Action or be Non=
suited, or Judgment shall be given against
him upon Demurrer or otherwise, then such
Defendant or Defendants shall have Treble
Costs to him or them Awarded against
such Plaintiff.

Provided always, and be it Enacted by
the Authority aforesaid, That all Infor=
mations, Actions and Suits to be brought
for any Offence against this Act shall be
Brought and Commenced within Twelve
Months after the Discovery of such Offence,
any former Law to the contrary thereof in
any wife notwithstanding.

And Whereas the Person or Persons who
make Seizure of the said Goods may be
hindred and delayed in the Prosecution there=
of by Vexatious Claims, being Entred
thereto, for the prevention whereof, Be it
Enacted

4

Enacted by the Authority aforesaid, That before any Person or Persons shall be admitted to Enter a Claim to any of the said Goods, he shall be Obliged to give good and sufficient Security by Recognizance to be entred into before one of the Barons of the Court of Exchequer, in the Penalty of Twenty Pounds, with Condition to Pay to the Officer or Person Prosecuting such Seizure his full Costs of Suit, in Case upon a Tryal or other Determination in Law, a Virdict shall pass or Judgment shall be Entred for the Plaintiff, and in case Default shall be made in giving such Security within the time limited by the Rules of the Court for Entring Claims, then the said Goods shall be Adjudged Forfeited, and Judgment Entred accordingly.

Provided always, and be it Enacted by the Authority aforesaid, That nothing in this Act contained shall Extend or be Construed to Extend to give Authority or Leave to any Person or Persons to Enter into any House, Shop, Cellar, Warehouse or other Room or Place, or to break open the same, or any Door, Chest, Trunk or other Package which does not belong to a Dealer in Lace.

F I N I S.

Queen Victoria

1819-1901 (reigned 1837-1901)

Queen Victoria's wedding lace

Queen Victoria's flounce was worn at her wedding in 1840. This lace flounce is of a very high standard both in workmanship and design. It was worked in the very fine cotton thread which is necessary to the production of such intricate and beautiful detail, but sadly this thread is unobtainable today. The flounce is still in excellent condition and measures 25½ inches deep by four yards in circumference.

Bold scrolls form the wide border at the base with exquisite vertical motifs rising from this. The flounce is densely patterned, consisting of many curved stems and leaves all outlined with much raised work. An unusual feature of the work is the variety of fillings that have been worked into the centre of the clothwork. Many of these are traditional and much-used today, but several are unusual and unknown to present day lacemakers. The fillings used consist chiefly of cushion, straight pin, diamond and brick but one unusual filling in the tulip-shaped flower has a snatch, four pin and spider – probably known as snatch pin spider.

The flounce is mounted on machine-made cotton net. This has been cut away underneath both the border and the large vertical motifs.

Queen Victoria's wedding flounce: detail 1

Queen Victoria's wedding flounce: detail 2

Queen Victoria's wedding flounce: detail 3

Queen Victoria's wedding flounce: detail 4

Queen Victoria's wedding flounce: detail 5

Queen Victoria's wedding flounce: detail 6

Queen Victoria's wedding flounce: detail 7

Queen Victoria's wedding flounce: detail 8

Queen Victoria's wedding flounce: detail 9

Queen Victoria's wedding flounce: detail 10

Queen Victoria's wedding flounce: detail 11

Queen Victoria's wedding flounce: detail 12

Queen Victoria's wedding veil is mounted on cotton net, and the size is approximately 18 inches deep at the corners varying to 8 inches at the sides. It is similar in design to that used for Queen Victoria's flounce, but with smaller flowers, leaves and scrolls. The work is, however, much lighter and more open in design, with a great variety of filling stitches used.

The corner design is almost completely connected by straight pin filling. Each flower has a variety of different fillings e.g. diamond, brick, cushion and wheels, and the standard of workmanship equals that of the flounce. Almost all parts are completely edged with ribbing, and the work was probably carried out by the same workers at Beer.

(*left*) Corner of Queen Victoria's wedding veil

(*this page*) Border of lace said to have been worn as a
cuff by Queen Victoria at her coronation. This shows a
view of one design which has been repeated for the cuff length.
The lace is partly raised, but is not as elaborate in design as the other
Royal laces. It has been mounted on machine net which has been cut away
beneath the filling stitches, and the fillings used are straight pin, swing and a
pin, and diamond.

The Royal Christening Robe

The Royal Christening Robe, made in 1841-2 for Queen Victoria of fine Honiton lace and lined with heavy cream silk, was worn at the christening of the infant Prince of Wales, later King Edward VII. In 1894 the robe was given by Queen Victoria to the Duchess of York, later Queen Mary, all of whose children were christened in it. It was also worn by the children of King George VI, the Duke of Gloucester and the Duke of Kent, and by the children of the Queen and Princess Margaret. It was worn by Prince William in 1982 and by Prince Henry in 1984.

Queen Victoria, Albert Edward, Prince of Wales (*left*), George, Duke of York and Prince Edward of York, after the latter's christening, 1894.

The Prince and Princess of Wales with Prince William wearing the Royal Christening Robe of Honiton lace, at his christening in 1982.

Full-length photograph of the Royal Christening Robe. The lace is of excellent design and workmanship. It contains a wealth of beautiful Honiton lace work which is still in good condition, but sadly the net background has become very delicate and fragile. It is lined with heavy cream silk and trimmed with ruched silk. The wide full-length sash hangs from the bodice with a fringe at the ends.

The bodice and sleeves of the Robe. These show a repeat pattern of the large centre spray design. The gown has lace cap sleeves.

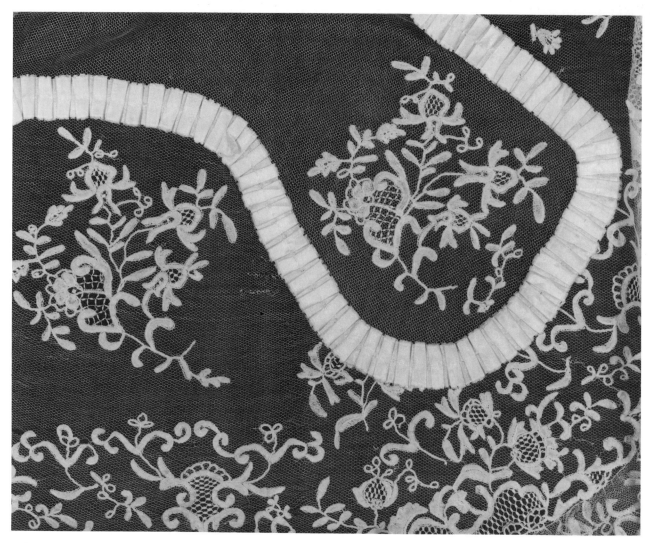

(*above*) The ruched silk trim each side of the centre spray.

(*right*) Full length close-up of the centre design, with open ribbed leaves and flowers. The net has been cut away beneath the leadwork fillings giving a light, dainty effect.

Close up photographs showing detail of the centre spray with repeats of the two fillings used.

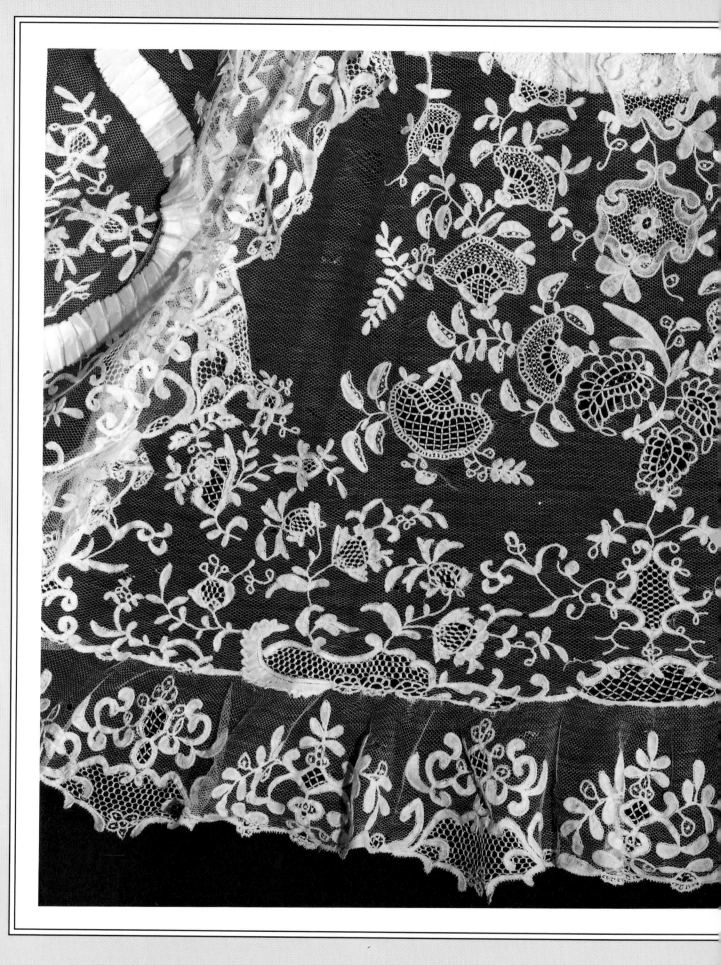

Lower edge border and base of centre flower with raised work. Diamond and brick fillings were used and the net has been cut away beneath all large and small fillings.

Princess Alexandra's wedding lace

Albert Edward, Prince of Wales, and Princess Alexandra of Denmark on their wedding day, 10 March 1863.

(for detail see over)

The wedding veil worn by Alexandra, Princess of Wales, at her wedding in 1863. The corner and sides of the veil are all bordered by a design of cornucopias; the same two fillings have been repeated in each – swing leadworks and blossom. Each design also contains a spray of roses, thistles and shamrock, with roses (the centre of each being diamond filling) connecting each cornucopia. Three of these have been arranged to form the corner of the veil with the repeats along each side, and the lace contains a wealth of raised work of excellent quality. The lace is mounted on machine net and has tiny thistles, roses and shamrock scattered over the inside net, interspersed with circles of rib.

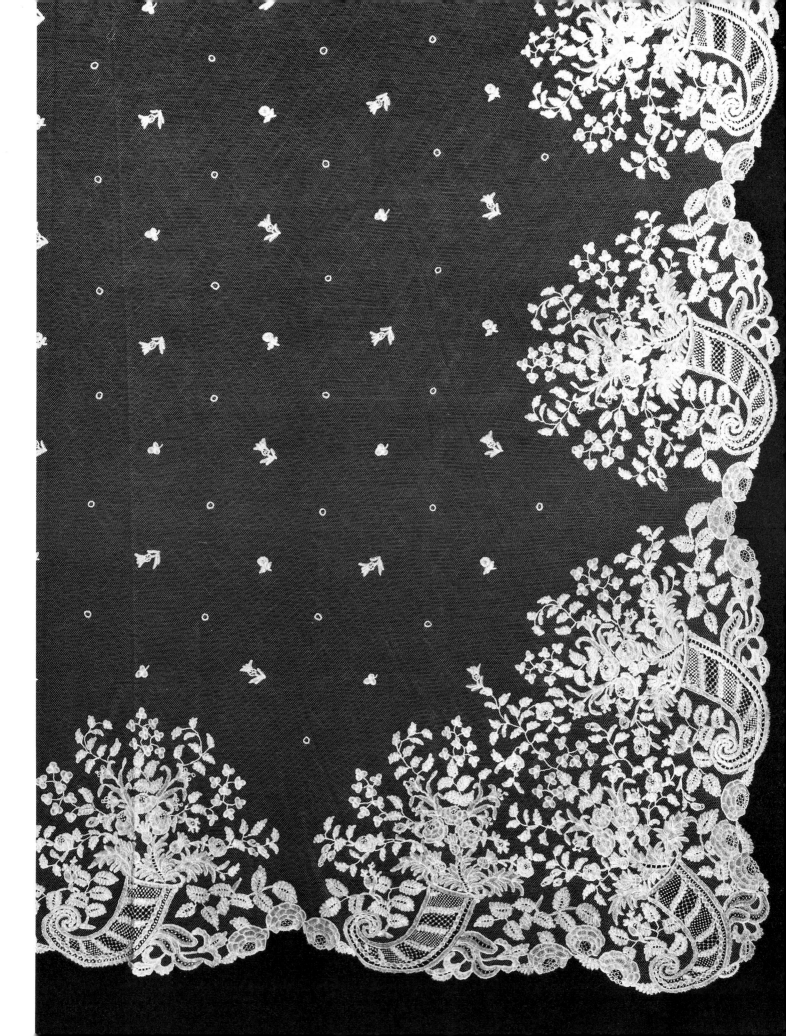

A flounce length from Princess Alexandra's bridal gown, repeating the same pattern as the veil i.e. cornucopias mounted on net with tiny circles of rib scattered on the background. It is recorded in Margaret Tomlinson's book *Three Generations in the Honiton Lace Trade* that all the lace was made or acquired by the Tucker family of Branscombe, and that four of these flounces were to be worn around the bridal gown.

Corner of the handkerchief which matches the veil and flounce of Alexandra,
Princess of Wales, and is said to have been carried by Mary Adelaide, Duchess
of Teck at the latter's wedding in 1866. In each corner of the handkerchief, the
cornucopia pattern has been reduced in size with smaller repeats of the sprays
(roses, thistles and shamrocks) along each of the sides.

(*above*) These show close-ups of the working of the pattern. Each petal of the flower, the leaves and the bud, has been completely raised and rolled. In the flower, the straight pin filling has been worked.

Baby outfit

(*on previous page*)

The photograph is of the complete baby gown which is Honiton appliqué on machine net. This gown was worn by the three children of Adolphus Frederick and Augusta, Duchess of Cambridge between 1819 and 1833. The floral spray has been repeated around the bottom of the gown and down the whole length of each side from hem to yoke, with repeat sprays across the yoke and on the tops of the small sleeves. The ribbon tie also has ends of lace with a repeat of the same flower. A tiny edging has been used for hem, sleeves, neckline and around the tie.

This matching baby cap (*opposite page*) has repeats of the pattern used on the gown, and consists of three lengths of lace mounted on a ground of drochel net – the whole joined together by ribbons with a ribbon tie.

Handkerchieves

This handkerchief is said to have been carried by Victoria Mary, Duchess of York at her wedding in 1893. The side and centre of the handkerchief show the embroidered monogram V and M with the crown above.

The lace consists of some raised and rolled work but has much flat work with simple repeats in the design – there are very few filling stitches used. The connecting of the sprays is made by purl bars only.

Two handkerchieves made for Victoria Mary, Duchess of York in 1893. Both are beautiful examples of raised and rolled Honiton lace. In the handkerchief on this page maple leaves are used on the corners and are repeated on the sides with flowers and tiny leaf sprays between each. Many repeats of raised leaves, flowers and cloth stitch trails are used. The fillings are diamond, brick and swing leadworks, and the motifs are joined by tiny purl bars to form the background of the lace. The initials 'V' and 'M' are embroidered on the centre linen beneath a crown.

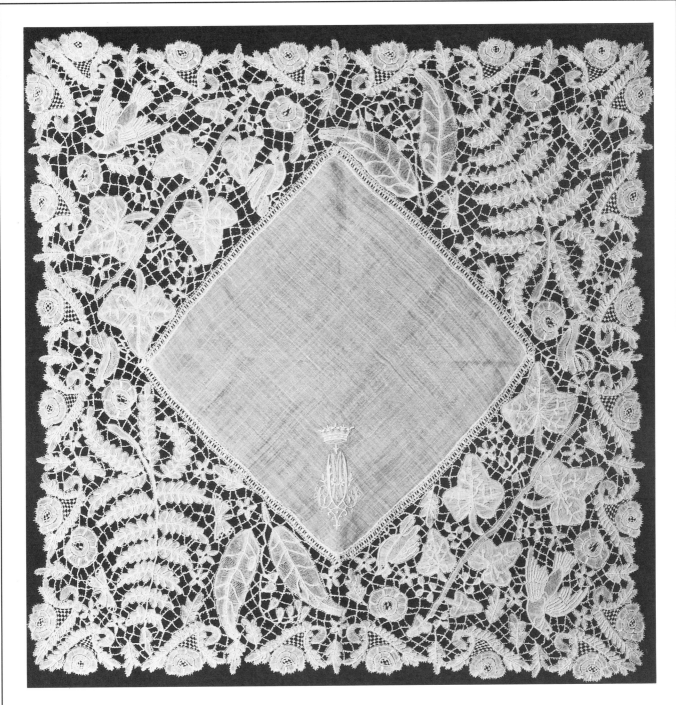

The handkerchief above also displays an excellent quality of workmanship. The fern leaves are raised and rolled, whilst the trails of ivy leaves have raised veins with wholestitch backing. Birds, butterflies and lily-of-the-valley sprays are included in the design. The corners and edges of the handkerchief consist of roses and tap leaves – the fillings being no pin and straight pin. Motifs are again joined by purl bars forming the background. As with the other handkerchief, the initials 'V' and 'M' with a crown have been embroidered on the linen inset – probably by the same worker.

The handkerchief made for the Brussels Exhibition of 1910 to the order of Queen Mary. This is indeed the most beautiful design and workmanship of all handkerchieves in the Royal collection. Only one corner and one side are shown here. The flowers are raised and rolled, and the centre of each has the toad-in-the-hole filling. The larger squared filling is not well known or made today; it has rib bars working into circles to form the corners of each square which contains one leadwork – the other corner fillings are purl bars. All the scrolls and flowers are raised, while the leaves have raised veins. The same pattern of flowers and leaves has been repeated for the sides of the handkerchief, while the background is handmade net.

The handkerchief presented to Queen Mary by the town of Honiton in 1911. A corner and one side are shown in the photograph. The corner design consists of a border of roses flanked at each side by thistles and shamrocks, and completed with much raised work. The thistle has a no pin filling backed with half-stitch, and the large thistle leaves are completely raised on the outer edge with open vein and leadworks. The main corner filling is straight pin, the remainder being net, whilst the side centre filling is swing and a pin. For the mounting on the linen the rolled method has been used.

The handkerchief given to Queen Mary in 1911. This consists mostly of flat work of traditional patterns with emblems of English roses. The corners have a thistle and shamrock design, while the remainder of the lace is made up of anchors, crowns, butterflies and the Prince of Wales feathers. Also included is the date 1911. The only filling used is diamond.

Pin cushion cover

Incorporated into this design are the Prince of Wales Feathers and the Royal Coat of Arms surrounded by convolvulus sprays, thistles and ivy leaves. Purl bars connect the pieces of lace, and there is an outer border of flowers.

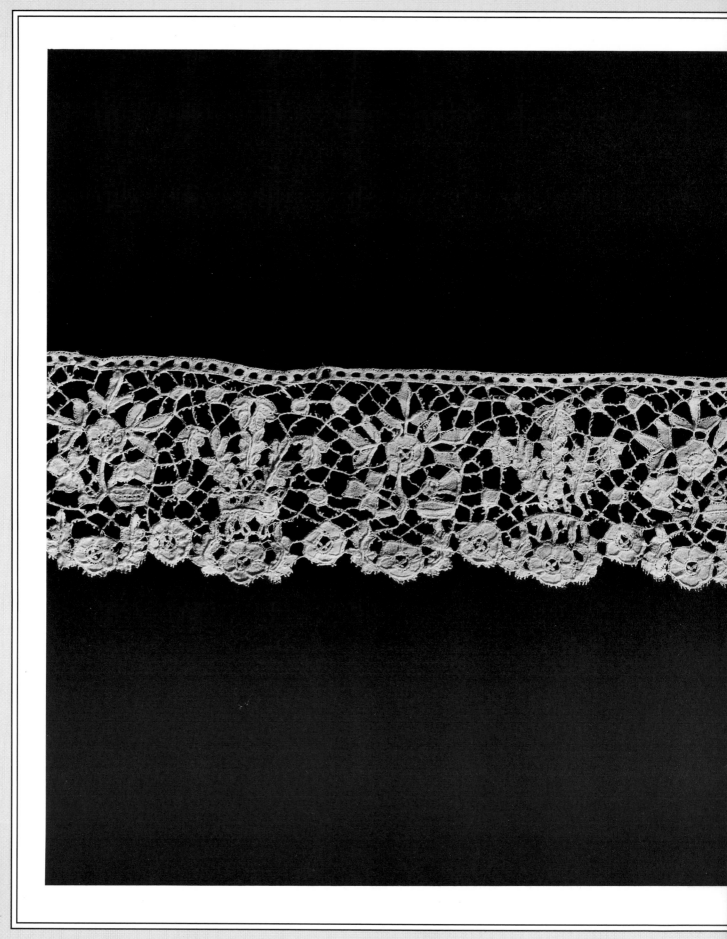

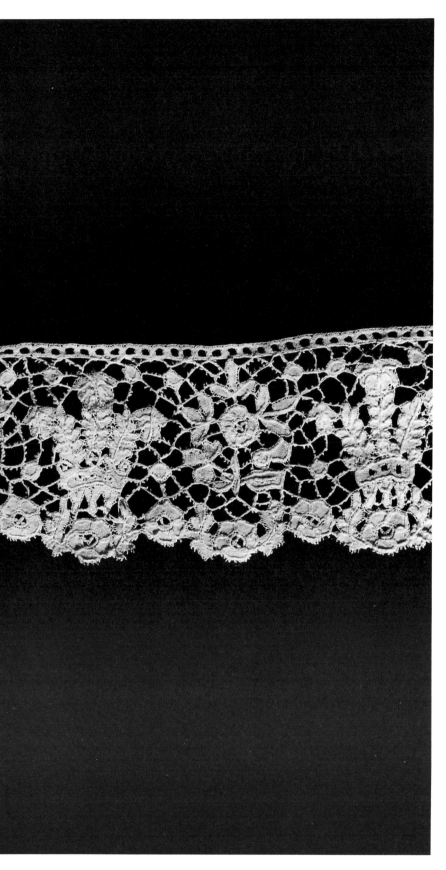

Border of Honiton guipure

The design consists of Prince of Wales Feathers, roses, thistles and shamrocks connected by purl bars.

Silk bags

The silk bag on this page is decorated with Honiton lace floral sprigs. The centre floral spray and the four surrounding birds consist of raised and rolled work. The lace is mounted on machine net, the outer edging having a small ribbed design.

The square silk bag above is decorated with a Honiton lace trail of leaves and
flowers. A crown and coat of arms form the centre. These are mounted on
machine net with a lining of silk and ribbon ties.

Wedding veil

The wedding veil belonging to Queen Elizabeth the Queen Mother. Its history and origin are unknown.

Corner of wedding veil: detail 1

Wedding veil: detail 2

Wedding veil: detail 3

Wedding veil: detail 4

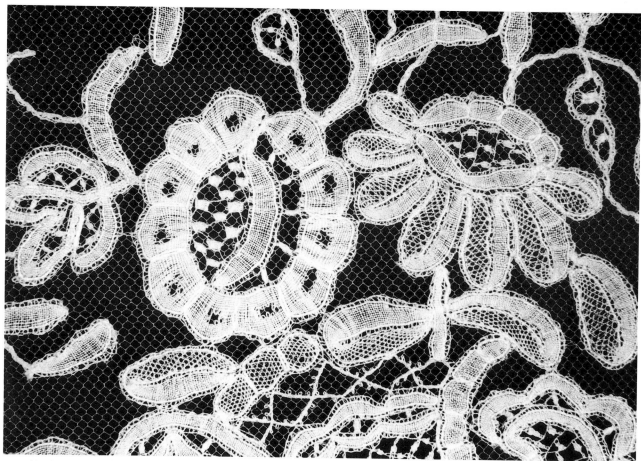

Wedding veil: detail 5

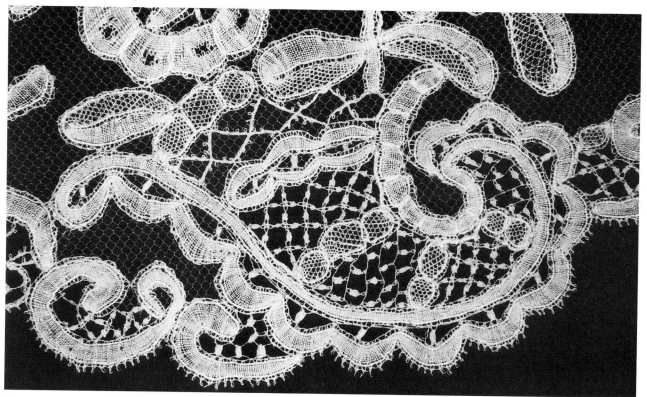

Wedding veil: detail 6

84

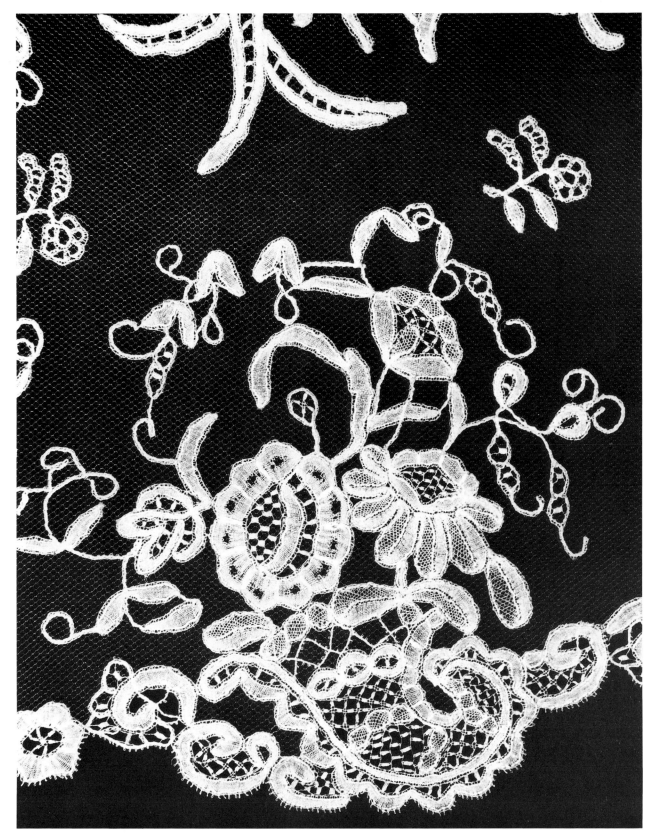

Wedding veil: detail 7

Queen Elizabeth the Queen Mother's coronation fan, 1936

Honiton lace in the mid-twentieth century*

Everyone knows of Honiton lace, but not one in a thousand knows that the best lace in Devon comes from the village of Beer, close to Seaton, for it is in Beer that the lace is made for the Queens of England. Actually, Honiton lace is a misnomer for most of it was, and is still, made in the surrounding villages, but it was all sent there for transport to London, and as it became the custom for merchants to send someone to meet the coaches bearing the boxes of lace from Honiton, the two gradually became identified with each other.

In 1840, Jane Bidney of Beer, was commissioned to make the bridal dress for the young Victoria. She gathered a hundred of the best lacemakers in the surrounding countryside to help her make the royal dress which cost £1000. So delighted was the Queen with its exquisite workmanship that she commanded Jane to attend her wedding.

Now, just on a century later, a descendant of Jane Bidney has made lace for another Queen of England, the fourth in succession, whose gracious patronage has shown an appreciation for this traditional local industry where beauty and exquisite craftsmanship are so happily united. This lace expert is Mrs Allen, of the Lace Shop, Beer, who was commanded by Queen Elizabeth to make some lace which was included in Her Majesty's wardrobe for the historic visit to Canada and the United States. This was the message which was conveyed to Mrs Allen by Lady Helen Graham, Lady-in-Waiting: 'The Queen directs me to say that she has greatly admired these specimens of lace and is deeply interested to know that this beautiful handicraft is still carried on by Devonshire workers as in the past'.

The Lace Shop, Beer, where the Royal Laces are restored

87

Queen Mary was another royal patroness whose commands were carried out by Mrs Allen and her clever assistants. Old lace needs very skilful handling when it has to be repaired or adapted for modern needs, and parcels of priceless old lace were sent from time to time by Queen Mary to the Lace Shop at Beer with instructions for repair which were faithfully and lovingly carried out by deft craftswomen.

It is not only Queens who like lace and fortunately, exquisite and delicate though the workmanship is, the price of Honiton lace is far from prohibitive. Today one may acquire at little cost a dainty trifle – perhaps a handkerchief or a collar – which will in its turn become an heirloom for another generation, and the bride whose veil comes from Beer will possess 'a thing of beauty' which may very possibly remain 'a joy for ever'.

*Reprinted from *Town and Country News* in which it appeared under the title, 'Where Lace is Made for Queens', 1950.

Jane Bidney in 1850

Modern lace

Six Honiton lace handkerchieves presented to Princess Margaret as a wedding gift from the National Federation of Women's Institutes in May 1960. Made by Devon lace teachers; the open centre handkerchief made by Elsie Luxton.

Honiton lace motif inscription ER 1952-1977. A gift from the town of Honiton to Queen Elizabeth II on the occasion of her Silver Jubilee.
Worked by Pat Perryman.

Prince of Wales Feathers. This was a wedding gift from the people of Honiton to Prince Charles and Lady Diana on 29 July 1981.
Worked by Pat Perryman.

Honiton lace Madonna presented to Queen Elizabeth II in March 1983 at the Maundy Service at Exeter Cathedral. Worked by Elsie Luxton and given by the Dean and Chapter of the Cathedral.

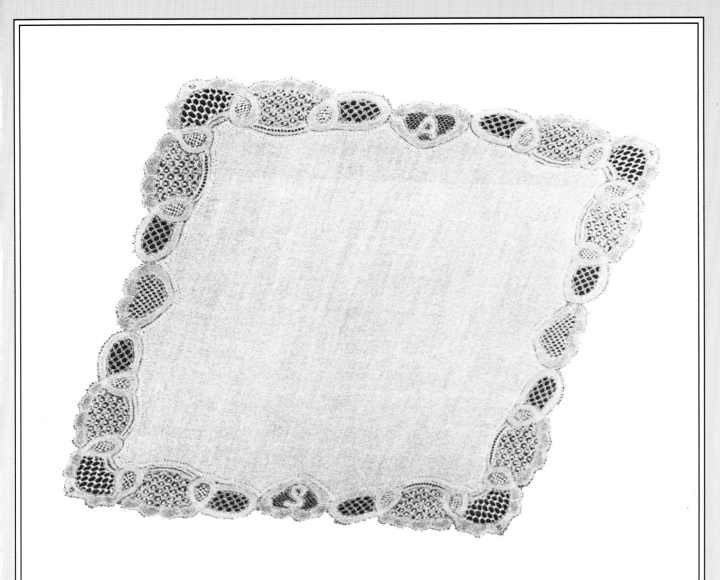

Honiton lace-edged handkerchief. A wedding gift to Prince Andrew and Miss Sarah Ferguson, the Duke and Duchess of York, 23 July 1986. Made and given by Elsie Luxton.

Further Reading

Treadwin, *Antique Point and Honiton Lace* (Ward Lock & Tyler, London, first published 1874)

Devonia, *The Honiton Lace Book* (The Bazaar Office, London, first published 1873; reprinted by Paul Minet, London, 1972)

Maidment, Margaret *A Manual of Hand-Made Bobbin Lace* (Charles T. Branford Co, Boston, 1954; reprinted by Piccadilly Rare Books, Paul Minet, London)

Palliser, *The History of Lace* (E. P. Publishing Ltd, first published 1902)

Penderel Moody, A. *Devon Pillow Lace* (Cassell & Co Ltd, first published 1907)

Luxton, Elsie *The Technique of Honiton Lace* (B.T. Batsford Ltd, first published 1979)

Luxton, Elsie *Honiton Lace Patterns* (B.T. Batsford Ltd, first published 1983)

Luxton, Elsie and Fukuyama, Yusai *Honiton Lace: The Visual Approach* (B.T. Batsford Ltd, first published 1988)

Levey, S.M. *Lace, A History* (Victoria & Albert Museum, 1983)

Index